SEASONS AND CELEBRATIONS

Thousands of years ago, people celebrated special times. New plants and animals in the spring, the longest day of summer, good food from the trees and fields in the autumn – these were all times to celebrate. Later, Christianity came, and old and new festivals came together as Easter, Christmas, and other celebrations.

Each season brings its own celebrations. Spring has eggs at Easter; in summer there are outside festivals at the summer solstice, and barbecues for the Fourth of July; autumn has fires and fireworks; and winter has the wonderful traditions of Christmas food and presents. But there are new celebrations too – Mother's Day, Remembrance Day, the special days of new countries, and the festivals that people bring with them when they move to different countries.

Here is a year of celebrations – old and new, inside and outside – in Britain, the USA, and other English-speaking countries. Learn about the traditions, read the stories – you can even cook the pancakes if you want!

OXFORD BOOKWORMS LIBRARY
Factfiles

Seasons and Celebrations

Stage 2 (700 headwords)

Factfiles Series Editor: Christine Lindop

This book is dedicated
to my wonderful husband Steve,
to my dear family and friends,
and to sufferers and survivors of breast cancer
everywhere around the world.
May you always have something to celebrate.

Jackie Maguire 1959-2007

JACKIE MAGUIRE

Seasons and Celebrations

OXFORD UNIVERSITY PRESS

OXFORD
UNIVERSITY PRESS

Great Clarendon Street, Oxford OX2 6DP

Oxford University Press is a department of the University of Oxford.
It furthers the University's objective of excellence in research, scholarship,
and education by publishing worldwide in

Oxford New York

Auckland Cape Town Dar es Salaam Hong Kong Karachi
Kuala Lumpur Madrid Melbourne Mexico City Nairobi
New Delhi Shanghai Taipei Toronto

With offices in

Argentina Austria Brazil Chile Czech Republic France Greece
Guatemala Hungary Italy Japan Poland Portugal Singapore
South Korea Switzerland Thailand Turkey Ukraine Vietnam

OXFORD and OXFORD ENGLISH are registered trade marks of
Oxford University Press in the UK and in certain other countries

© Oxford University Press 2008

The moral rights of the author have been asserted

Database right Oxford University Press (maker)

22

ISBN: 978 0 19 423383 5

A complete recording of this Bookworms edition of
Seasons and Celebrations is available.

Printed in China

Word count (main text): 6508

For more information on the Oxford Bookworms Library, visit www.oup.com/elt/bookworms

The publishers would like to thank the following for their permission to reproduce images:
Alamy Images pp 3 David Robertson, 5 Mary Evans Picture Library, 9 Mary Evans Picture Library,
10 David Hancock, 15 Tim Mossford, 17 Gary Roebuck, 22 Mary Evans Picture Library, 23 Robert
Harding Picture Library Ltd, 24 Michael Perris, 34 Janine Wiedel Photolibrary, 35 Bill Bachman,
36 Barry Lewis, 40 Adrian Sherratt; Anthony Blake Photo Library pp 12 Sian Irvine, 14 (Easter
egg/Heather Brown), 14 (Hot cross buns/Sue Atkinson), 30 Maximilian Stock Ltd, 38 (Christmas
table/Graham Kirk); Corbis pp 11 Paul A. Souders, 18 BBC, 29 (Anzac Dawn service/Reuters/David
Gray), 31 Bettmann; Getty Images pp 8 Reportage, 20 Reportage/Peter Macdiarmid, 25 Mel Yates,
27 The Bridgeman Art Library/ Trelleek, 32 Stone/John E Kelly; OUP p 50 Ingram; PunchStock pp
viii (Petifours), 38 (cracker); Rex Features pp 4 Andrew Drysdale, 6 Sarah Arar, 29 (Queen Elizabeth
/Tim Rooke)

Cover image by Alamy Images / Eyebyte

CONTENTS

1 Festivals old and new

The people of Britain have had festivals for thousands of years. Long ago the sun, the moon, the wind, rain, animals, and trees were all important in their religions, and they had festivals for them. When Christianity came to Britain, people wanted to keep some of their old festivals so they brought the religions together. Saint Valentine's Day, Easter, Halloween, and Christmas are all old festivals that became Christian festivals.

Food, family, and flowers are an important part of most celebrations. Most people have a big family dinner at Christmas, and many people get together at Thanksgiving too. A lot of people give chocolate and other sweets as presents on Valentine's Day and at Easter and Christmas, and some festivals have special food. Restaurants are very busy on Valentine's Day and Mother's Day, and flower shops sell a lot of flowers on those days.

People today often live far away from their families, so they send cards at special times like Mother's Day, Easter and Christmas. The cards say things like: 'Thinking of you across the miles'. Post offices and telephones are very busy too, and many people use their phones and computers to send messages.

Times change, and festivals also change. People have celebrated many of these festivals for hundreds of years, and will go on finding new ways to enjoy them.

2   The year begins

New Year's Eve is on 31 December, the last day before the New Year begins. In many places, people go to parties or restaurants with friends in the evening. Sometimes they meet outside: in New York, thousands of people go to Times Square; in Sydney they go down near the sea; in London, they go to Trafalgar Square. Just before midnight, people look at the clock, and together they count the last ten seconds before the New Year begins: 'Ten, nine, eight . . . '

At midnight they stand in a circle, hold hands and sing an old song called *Auld Lang Syne*. A Scottish man called Robert Burns wrote the words of this song about two hundred years ago. The song says that it is good to remember your old friends. Then many people drink a glass of champagne, light some fireworks, or dance until the sun comes up.

In Scotland, New Year's Eve has a special name: Hogmanay. At Hogmanay, there is a tradition called first-footing. The first person to come into the house in the New Year is the 'first-foot': if he is a tall man with dark hair, he will bring good luck to the house. He must carry some food, some money, or a piece of black coal for the fire.

In Edinburgh and other Scottish cities, there are house parties and street parties, Scottish music and dancing,

Fireworks on Hogmanay in Edinburgh

parades and lots of fireworks. Sometimes the parties go on all night and into the next day.

New Year's Day, 1 January, is a holiday for most people, and the banks and many shops do not open. Many people stay at home and rest on that day. And a lot of people

January sales

make a New Year's resolution. This means that they decide to do something different because they want to be a better person. For example, they say: 'I'm going to stop smoking,' or 'I'm going to eat better,' or 'I'm going to learn something new.'

After the holiday the shops are very busy with January sales. At sale time things in the shops are cheaper – sometimes much cheaper – so it is a good time to go shopping. And when people do go out, they usually say 'Happy New Year!' when they see friends and family for the first time in January.

A few weeks later it is Valentine's Day. This started more than two thousand years ago, as a winter festival, on 15 February. On that day, people asked their gods to give them good fruit and vegetables, and strong animals.

When the Christians came to Britain, they came with a story about a man called Saint Valentine. The story is that Valentine was a Christian who lived in Rome in the

third century. The Roman Emperor at the time, Claudius the Second, was not a Christian. Claudius thought that married soldiers did not make good soldiers, so he told his soldiers that they must not marry. Valentine worked for the church, and one day he helped a soldier who wanted to marry. The Emperor said that Valentine had to die because of this, and he sent Valentine to prison. But Valentine fell in love with the daughter of a man who worked there. Just before he died, he sent a note to this woman, and at the end of the note, he wrote: 'Your Valentine.' He died on 14 February, so the date of the festival changed from 15 to 14 February and the name changed to Saint Valentine's Day.

In the early nineteenth century people started to give Valentine's cards to the person they loved on 14 February. The cards had pictures of birds and flowers on them – perhaps red roses, the flower of love – and inside there were words like these:

Won't you be my Valentine

Roses are red, my love,
Violets are blue
Sugar is sweet, my love,
But not as sweet as you.

Choosing roses for Valentine's Day

People still send each other Valentine's cards, but often they do not write their names inside: they just write 'Be my Valentine,' or 'From your Valentine'.

Some children give their friends or teachers cards or chocolates. A man will perhaps give red roses to the woman that he loves. A lot of people go out to restaurants for the evening and have dinner for two, and some people think it is a good day to marry.

3   National days

Most countries have a day that is special to them – a national day. For England, Scotland, Wales, and Ireland the national day is the day that belongs to their patron saint. This is someone from the church who is important for a group of people; Saint Christopher, for example, is the patron saint of travellers.

The first of these four national days is 1 March. Saint David (Dewi Sant in the Welsh language) is the patron saint of Wales and 1 March is Saint David's Day. David and his followers lived quietly in Wales; they did not eat meat, and they drank only water. David became a famous teacher and a very important man in the church in Wales. He died in 589.

The Welsh love music and singing, so there are many concerts around the country on this day.

Next is 17 March, Saint Patrick's Day, which is a big day in Ireland and also in North America. Saint Patrick was born in about 385. He travelled all over Ireland, teaching and talking to people about Christianity. He also built a lot of schools and churches there. He died on 17 March 461.

On Saint Patrick's Day there are parades, church services and festivals in Dublin, Belfast and many other Irish towns and cities. But it is also an important day in the USA. In the nineteenth century a lot of Irish people

A Saint Patrick's Day parade

travelled to the USA to begin a new life. Saint Patrick's Day was very important to them, because it was a day to remember Ireland. The Saint Patrick's Day Parade in New York is now one of the biggest parades in the world. There are parties in other places all over the USA and Canada too. Some people wear green clothes, some drink lots of beer – and some even drink green beer!

Saint George is the patron saint of England, and 23 April is Saint George's Day. He was a Christian and a soldier in the Roman army in the third century. When the Roman Emperor Diocletian said that people could not follow the Christian religion any more, George said that he would not stop being a Christian. Diocletian was very angry, and told his soldiers to torture and then kill George, and he died in the year 303. One famous story about him is that he killed a dragon that ate people. Pictures of Saint George often show him on a horse, killing a dragon.

Saint George became the patron saint of England in the fourteenth century in the time of King Edward the

Third. In 1348 King Edward shouted 'Saint George for England!' when he took his men to war. Most English people do not do anything special on this day but some are trying to make it a more important day. In the city of Salisbury there has been a parade on Saint George's Day since King Edward's time.

Saint Andrew is the patron saint of Scotland and 30 November is Saint Andrew's Day. Saint Andrew was probably a fisherman in Galilee and took Christianity to Greece. One story says that the Romans killed him there. Someone moved his body to Istanbul in Turkey and then to Scotland. They left the body in the place that is now the city called Saint Andrews.

Saint George and the dragon

Scotland celebrates Saint Andrew's Day with concerts and ceilidhs – parties with traditional music and dancing. Scots who live in other countries often meet on this day and think about family and friends far away.

In other countries the national day is often on the date of something important that happened there. In Australia that day is 26 January: Australia Day. On that day in 1788 the first British ships arrived in the place that is now called Sydney. The Australia Day Regatta, a celebration with lots of sailing races, began in 1837, and still happens in Sydney every year. There are lots of other celebrations all over the country. But not everybody is happy about Australia Day. Many Aboriginal Australians – the first people of Australia – do not celebrate this day.

The Australia Day Regatta

Maori dancers on Waitangi Day

New Zealand's national day is on 6 February and is called Waitangi Day. On 6 February 1840 people from the British government met a group of Maori chiefs in Waitangi in the north of New Zealand. They all put their names on an important paper called the Treaty of Waitangi, which said that New Zealand was now a British colony. On 6 February every year there is a celebration at Waitangi, and there are lots of celebrations, concerts, and festivals in other places. But not all Maori are happy about the Treaty of Waitangi or the celebrations.

Canada Day is 1 July. On that day people remember the day in 1867 when the British North America colonies became the Dominion of Canada. There are celebrations all over the country, with pancake breakfasts, barbecues, parades, music, and fireworks. The biggest celebrations are in Ottawa, home of the Canadian government: it's a great day to visit the city!

4   Lent and Easter

Easter is the most important festival in the church year, more important than Christmas. People begin to get ready for Easter forty days before Easter Sunday. These forty days are called Lent, and they begin on Ash Wednesday. The day before Ash Wednesday is Pancake Day.

During Lent, some Christians stop eating a favourite food, like sugar or chocolate. In the past, people traditionally stopped eating eggs and milk. So just before Lent began, they took all their eggs and milk and made thin round cakes called pancakes. People eat pancakes in different ways in different countries, but in Britain they usually have them with lemon juice and sugar.

To make about twelve pancakes, you need:

125g flour
Salt (just a little)
1 egg
300ml milk
Butter
Sugar
Lemon juice

Put the flour and salt in a big bowl.
Make a hole in the middle and break the egg into it.
Use a fork to mix it all together.
Slowly mix the milk into the egg and flour.

Make your pan hot, then put some butter in it.

Put two big spoons of the mix into the pan to make a thin pancake.

Cook for about half a minute, then turn the pancake over (toss it if you are feeling clever!).

Put the pancake on a plate, and keep it warm while you cook the other pancakes.

Eat your pancake with a little lemon juice and sugar.

Thirty-eight days after Pancake Day is Good Friday. On this day the Romans killed Jesus Christ in Jerusalem, about two thousand years ago. Christians think that Jesus came back to life two days later, on Easter Sunday.

Easter is now a Christian festival but the word 'Easter' comes from 'Eostre', the old name for the goddess of spring. Easter Day is the Sunday after the first full moon after the first day of spring (21 March). It is always between 22 March and 25 April.

Many animals and birds are born in the spring, so when people started to send Easter cards in the nineteenth century, the cards often had baby sheep, rabbits, or chickens on them.

Eggs are an important part of Easter because they mean spring and new life. On Easter Sunday, people give chocolate Easter eggs as presents. This tradition started in Europe in the early nineteenth century and came to Britain in the 1870s. Some mothers and fathers tell their children that the Easter Rabbit brings the eggs and hides them in the garden, and that the children must go outside and look for them.

Easter eggs

Many people also eat hot cross buns at Easter. These are a kind of bread, made with fruit and spices, and they have a white cross (+) on top. You eat them hot with butter. There is an old song about them:

Hot cross buns, hot cross buns,
One a penny, two a penny,
Hot cross buns.
If you have no daughters,
Give them to your sons,
One a penny, two a penny,
Hot cross buns.

Hot cross buns

An Easter bonnet

Some women and children decorate hats, called Easter bonnets. They put lots of spring flowers, rabbits, or chickens on them, and wear them in Easter bonnet parades. And of course many people go to church on Easter Day. There are lots of flowers in the churches and people sing special Easter songs.

Easter Monday is a holiday for most people, so many watch some sport or go out for the day. Children usually have one or two weeks' holiday from school around Easter.

5   Families and fools

In Britain the fourth Sunday of Lent was called Mothering Sunday. Centuries ago, people visited the 'mother' church in their town or village on this day. Later, when young people started to leave home to work, and live farther away, they had a day's holiday once a year to visit their mother and the mother church. They took presents like flowers or cake home to their mothers. Slowly, Mothering Sunday changed to Mother's Day – a special day for mothers.

During the Second World War (1939–1945), many American soldiers in Britain stayed with British families and gave their British 'mothers' presents on Mothering Sunday. But in the USA Mother's Day is on a different day.

An American woman called Anna Jarvis had a special service in her church to remember her mother when she died. She wanted to have a special day for mothers, and many people agreed that it would be a good thing. Anna's mother died on the second Sunday in May, and Anna wanted that day to be Mother's Day. She talked to business people and people in the government about her plan for a special day all over the USA. In 1914, President Woodrow Wilson said that the second Sunday in May would be Mother's Day across the USA. It is also that day in Canada, Australia, and New Zealand.

Children try to do things to say 'thank you' to their

mothers on that day; they give them breakfast in bed, or take them out for a meal, or give them a present.

People have also celebrated Father's Day for about a hundred years. Many people wanted to thank their

A present for Mother's Day

fathers for all their hard work, help and love too. The first Father's Day was in the USA in 1910. In 1966, American President Lyndon Johnson said that the third Sunday in June would be Father's Day across the USA. It is the same day in Britain and Canada, but in Australia and New Zealand it is the first Sunday in September. On Father's Day people often like to take their father out, for example for a meal or to watch or do some sport.

After Mother's Day comes April, and April Fool's Day. How did April Fool's Day begin? Until the middle of the sixteenth century, France celebrated the new year on 1 April. Then in 1564, King Charles the Ninth decided to change this, and the new year began on 1 January. The message about this change travelled through the country very slowly, and some people did not know about the change or did not like it. When these people tried to give new year presents on 1 April, other people laughed at them and called them 'fools' or stupid people. After this,

Spaghetti trees on TV in 1957

1 April was called All Fool's Day, and later April Fool's Day. In many countries it became a day to play jokes on people and laugh at them.

Some people play little jokes on their friends and family; perhaps they change the time on the clocks, or put salt in the sugar bowl so someone's tea tastes terrible. Some play jokes on thousands of people on this day. In 1957, the BBC (British Broadcasting Corporation) showed a television programme about Swiss spaghetti trees. At that time, not many people ate spaghetti in Britain – it was a new food – so they did not know much about it. On the programme women took spaghetti from trees and put it in the sun to dry. When the programme finished, a lot of people telephoned the BBC. They all wanted to buy spaghetti trees for their gardens!

In 1998 there was Burger King's new hamburger. Millions of people in the USA usually use their left hand to write with, and the left-handed hamburger was for them! Thousands of people went to Burger King to get a left-handed hamburger – and thousands of others asked for 'a right-handed hamburger please – not a left-handed one'. The next year Burger King played the same joke in Britain – and the same thing happened.

In 2005 another British TV programme told people about 'fruitshakes' – a fruit and milk drink. The makers of fruitshakes gave their cows fruit to eat, and the cows gave them a milk drink that tasted of fruit.

Every year there are new jokes – on TV, in the newspapers, and on the radio. And every year millions of people think that the stories are true.

6 Summer celebrations

The longest day of the year is called the summer solstice. In Britain, it is usually on 21 June, which is the first day of summer. The word solstice comes from two Latin words: 'sol', which means sun, and 'sistere', which means to stand still.

Summer was always a good season for people in the past, because it was easy to find food. It was also a good time to find sweet honey, so the first full moon in June is called the honey moon. Many men and women marry in June, and the holiday that people take after they marry is still called the honeymoon.

At Stonehenge and Avebury in Wiltshire, England, there are some special circles made of big heavy stones which have been there for about five thousand years. How did they get there? Why are they there? Who put them

The summer solstice at Stonehenge

there? There are lots of different answers to these questions, but nobody can really be sure.

Because the summer solstice is traditionally a time of sun, light, food, love, and hot weather, people come from all over England to Stonehenge and Avebury on 21 June to celebrate. Some of the visitors are Druids, who follow an old pagan religion, older than Christianity; some are travellers, who like to move around the country and live in lots of different places; and some just want to stay up all night and then watch the sun come up in a very famous, old and interesting place.

Soon after the summer solstice there is an important date in the USA – the Fourth of July. During the seventeenth and eighteenth centuries, many people sailed from Britain to North America and started a new life there. New homes like this in other countries were called colonies. The British king was still king of the people in the colonies, and so they had to send taxes to Britain every year. But the thirteen American colonies wanted to be free from Britain: they wanted their government to be

in America. They did not want to send money to Britain, and many people became very angry about this.

In 1770 British soldiers shot some of these people in Boston, and in 1773 there was the famous Boston Tea Party. A tea ship came to Boston and there was a fight about the taxes on the tea. Three hundred and forty big boxes of tea went into the water! Now King George the Third and his government were angry too.

On 4 July 1776, the United States government in Philadelphia agreed to the Declaration of Independence. This said that the United States was a free, or independent, country, and that George the Third was not its king any more. Now it was war. The British and the Americans fought each other until 1781, when the Americans won. In 1783 the United States of America was born.

The first Fourth of July celebration was in Philadelphia

The Boston Tea Party

A Fourth of July parade

in 1777, during the war. There were guns, parades, fireworks, music, and a lot of noise. Now, every year on the Fourth of July, Americans celebrate Independence Day.

There are special church services at this time, but most of the celebrations are outside because it is summer. Many families have a barbecue, eat, and play games in their gardens or in a park.

In many towns, there are parades through the streets with loud music and lots of bright colours. The red, white and blue American flag flies everywhere. It has fifty white stars and thirteen stripes (seven red, six white). The fifty stars are for the fifty states in the United States, and the thirteen stripes are for the first thirteen states – the colonies. The flag has changed many times but today's flag goes back to the Fourth of July 1960, when Hawaii became the fiftieth state.

Independence Day usually ends with lots of fireworks. It is like one big party.

7 Fires and fireworks

The pagans who lived in Britain two thousand years ago celebrated their New Year on 1 November. Then the Christians came and people celebrated Hallowmas, a three-day festival between 31 October and 2 November. 31 October was called All Hallow's Eve and slowly the name changed to Halloween.

In November, winter is near, and hundreds of years

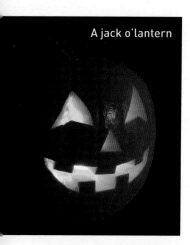

A jack o'lantern

ago people thought that bad spirits, like ghosts, came in the winter. They wanted the bad spirits to go away, so they made fires outside and made jack o'lanterns. To do this they took a big autumn vegetable – usually a pumpkin – and cut off the top. They made a big hole inside the pumpkin and cut a face in the side. Then they put a light inside the pumpkin and put the top on again. People still enjoy doing this today. You can see jack o'lanterns, with their bright eyes and mouths, outside at Halloween.

To keep the bad spirits away people also dressed like witches and ghosts. Children still do this if they go to Halloween parties. People often put up decorations for

Halloween parties, and play games. The decorations are usually black (for dark nights and death) and orange (for the autumn vegetables).

One Halloween party game is called 'bobbing for apples'. Many apples fall off the trees in autumn so they are easy to find. Someone puts some apples in a big bowl of water. The apples stay on top of the water. The first player often puts something over their eyes so they cannot see. They must keep their hands behind their back and take an apple out of the water with their teeth. Then the next player tries. It can be very difficult and players usually get very wet!

In Canada and the USA, and in some other English-speaking countries, children go 'trick or treating'. They dress like witches and ghosts, and go, often in a small group, to the houses of people who live near them. When someone answers the door, the children say: 'Trick or treat?' Then the person in the house must decide. Either they give the children a treat – something nice, like fruit or chocolate – or the children play a trick on them. For a trick, the children do

Trick or treating on Halloween

something bad like throw an egg or some flour at the house!

November brings more fires and fireworks. Sometimes you will hear people say, 'Remember, remember, the fifth of November'; they are talking about Guy Fawkes Night.

The story of Guy Fawkes Night begins in 1605. At that time James the First was King of England. But some people did not want him to be king, because they followed a different religion from James. So a group of them – a man called Guy Fawkes and his friends – made a plot to kill King James and his government at the Houses of Parliament in London on 5 November 1605.

They put thirty-six boxes of gunpowder in a room underneath the Houses of Parliament because they wanted to kill a lot of people. But the plan did not work. One of the plotters wrote a note to someone about it. At about midnight on 4 November, the King's soldiers found Guy Fawkes and the gunpowder. They sent him to prison but he did not want to give the names of his friends. They tortured him, and five days later he said all their names.

Some of the plotters tried to escape, but in January 1606 Guy Fawkes and some of his friends were killed in front of the Houses of Parliament. When people heard that the plotters were dead, they celebrated with lots of fires in the streets. King James was alive and well!

Since that time, every year on 5 November in most parts of Britain people build a big fire outside, with all the dead leaves and old pieces of wood that they do not want. The fire is called a bonfire. Children push newspaper into old clothes to make something that looks like a man.

They call it a 'guy', after Guy Fawkes, and sometimes they carry the guy around the streets to show people. They say: 'Penny for the guy', and ask people for money for fireworks.

Some people have a bonfire with fireworks in their garden, but fireworks are expensive, so often people have one big party together in a park or a field. It is usually very cold in November, so they have hot food and drinks to keep warm.

And every year, before the government comes to the Houses of Parliament, people go through the building and look carefully for gunpowder!

Guy Fawkes

8 Remembering

In November, near the end of the year, it is time to remember. On 11 November 1918, the First World War came to an end, and now 11 November has become Remembrance Day.

An Australian man called Edward George Honey wrote to the London Evening News in 1919. In his letter he said he wanted people to stop on one day and think about the soldiers who died in the war. King George the Fifth saw the letter and agreed, so he asked everyone to stop work and remember the dead. And so in the UK and other countries people are silent for two minutes at the eleventh hour of the eleventh day of the eleventh month. They stop everything and wait silently, in schools, streets, shopping centres and even big busy airports.

The nearest Sunday to 11 November is Remembrance Sunday. In towns and cities soldiers young and old walk together in parades to remember the soldiers who died in all the different wars. There are church services and special music, and at the war memorials, which have the names of dead soldiers on them, people put flowers. In London, the Queen and the Prime Minister put flowers on the big war memorial called the Cenotaph.

At this time of year many people wear red paper flowers called poppies. Why? During the First World War, hundreds of thousands of soldiers died on the fields of

The Queen on
Remembrance Sunday

Flanders, in Belgium. Later, thousands of poppies grew in the same fields. The beautiful red flowers were the colour of blood. When people buy the paper poppies today, the money helps old soldiers and their families.

In the USA, this day is called Veterans Day, while in Australia and New Zealand the important day is ANZAC Day, on 25 April. On this day in 1915 a big group of soldiers from these two countries, called the Australia and New Zealand Army Corps, arrived in Gallipoli in Turkey. About 11,000 of them died there. All the soldiers who fought at Gallipoli are dead now, but there are still services on ANZAC Day early in the morning. When the sun comes up, people remember the young ANZAC soldiers at Gallipoli, and other soldiers who have died in wars.

ANZAC Day in Australia

9　Thanksgiving

Most fruit and vegetables grow through the summer. When autumn comes, it is time to bring them in from the trees and fields. This time is called the harvest. After the harvest, many people want to say thank you for all the food. There are church services called Harvest Festivals or Thanksgiving Services. There are lots of vegetables, fruit, flowers, and bread in the church, and people sing special songs of thanks. These services started hundreds of years ago.

In September 1620, a group of English people called the Pilgrim Fathers sailed from Plymouth, England across

Autumn fruits, vegetables, and flowers

the Atlantic Ocean, in a ship called the *Mayflower*, to Cape Cod in North America. They went away from England because they did not agree with the religion in England. They wanted to make a new life in a new country.

They sailed for sixty-six dangerous days across the Atlantic Ocean. When they arrived, they called their new home New England, but they were not the first people to live there. The Wampanoag were the first people. Sometimes the Pilgrim Fathers fought with the Wampanoag, but they also learned a lot from them. The Wampanoag taught them to live from their new land, and to grow and cook new kinds of fruit and vegetables.

The first winter was difficult. Many of the Pilgrim Fathers died because it was very cold and they had little food. In the spring they started to grow food, with the help of some friendly Wampanoag, and in the autumn of

The Pilgrim Fathers

1621 they celebrated their first harvest. They gave thanks, not only for the harvest, but for their new home, new life and new friends.

Thanksgiving Day is the fourth Thursday in November. Canada is north of the USA, so the winter is longer and the harvest is earlier there. The date of Thanksgiving Day there is the second Monday in October. Most American and Canadian families still have a Thanksgiving Day dinner together. They have turkey and autumn vegetables, and then pumpkin pie.

In the USA, it is an important day for American football. Many people go to watch football or stay at home and watch it on television.

A Thanksgiving Day dinner

10 In a new country

In the last few centuries many people have moved to other countries taking their language and religion with them, just like the Pilgrim Fathers. People of different cultures have also come to live in English-speaking countries, bringing their festivals and celebrations with them. Today children in countries like Britain, Canada, the USA, Australia, and New Zealand learn about other people's special days from a young age. They learn about religious celebrations such as Jewish Hanukkah, Hindu Diwali and Muslim Eid, and they learn about other sides of people's cultures too.

There are many festivals which celebrate the culture of different groups of immigrants – people who have come to another country to live. One famous festival is the Notting Hill Carnival in London at the end of August. Immigrants from the Caribbean began the carnival in the 1960s. At first it was a small street festival with a few people in colourful clothes and some Caribbean music, but it got bigger and bigger. Now a million or more people come to see the carnival on the streets of London every summer.

There is also the Brick Lane Festival in a part of London sometimes called 'Banglatown' because there are so many people from Bangladesh there. This area is famous for its restaurants and great food, and for the many immigrants who have lived there over the years.

The Brick Lane Festival, London

Canada has Multiculturalism Day on 27 June, with celebrations of the food, music and dance of many immigrant groups all across the country. In the USA, there are many African-American festivals, and Spanish speakers from Latin American countries have started Hispanic American Festivals in many cities.

Most big cities in the USA have Chinatowns where a lot of Chinese immigrants live. San Francisco's Chinatown is the biggest outside of Asia. Sydney and Melbourne in Australia have big Chinatowns too – great places to eat Chinese food and see colourful celebrations of Chinese New Year with parades, dragons, and fireworks. And in Auckland, New Zealand they have the Asia:NZ Lantern

Festival. This celebrates both Chinese New Year and the cultures of the many immigrants who came to New Zealand from Asia.

So times change, and the traditions of the old country become part of the celebrations of the new country.

Chinese New Year in Melbourne, Australia

11 Christmas

Then December comes, and children begin to get excited because of Christmas. About two thousand years ago, Jesus was born in the town of Bethlehem. At Christmas, people remember that special time. Today, Christmas is a very important time in the Christian year, but it is also very important to people who do not go to church. It is a time for presents, parties, and time with the family.

People start to get ready for Christmas in late October or early November. They decorate their shops with lights, trees, and other decorations. Shops get very busy and stay open later. People with family and friends in other

A Christmas play at school

countries often send them cards and presents, and everyone begins to make plans for the coming holiday. Some people begin to look for presents too.

In the middle of December, most families buy Christmas trees, put them inside the house, and put colourful decorations on them. They also send cards to friends and family. The cards say things like 'Merry Christmas and a Happy New Year' or 'Season's Greetings'. These two traditions (the trees and the cards) both started in the nineteenth century.

Many children learn about the baby Jesus at school. Sometimes they do a play about the story and sing Christmas songs, called carols, for their mothers and fathers. A lot of schools have parties for the children, and many adults have parties at work in December. Most people do not have to work on 25 and 26 December, and many have a week's holiday, from 25 December to 1 January. They usually spend this time at home with their family, or perhaps they visit friends or family who live far away.

The Christmas holiday begins on 24 December: Christmas Eve. People often stop work early and have a drink together, or finish their Christmas shopping. They put special Christmas paper on the presents and leave them under the tree.

Children leave a stocking for Santa Claus (called Father Christmas in Britain) when they go to bed. Santa is a big man with white hair and red clothes who brings presents for children during the night. Mothers and fathers tell their children that Santa only comes when they are sleeping. They also tell them that Santa leaves presents

Pulling crackers

for good children – but for bad children he only leaves a piece of black coal! The children are excited, of course, so often they do not sleep very well. Some children leave a drink and a mince pie for Santa and some vegetables for his animals.

Many people go to church at midnight on Christmas

Christmas pudding and mince pies

Eve. They listen to the Christmas story and sing carols. Next morning it is Christmas Day – 25 December. Children usually wake up very early. They look in their stockings to see the presents that Santa put there for them. After breakfast they open their other presents around the tree.

Christmas dinner is in the afternoon and is the biggest meal of the day. Before they start to eat, people pull crackers. The crackers make a loud noise, and have a small game and a paper hat inside. Dinner is usually turkey with lots of winter vegetables and then a Christmas pudding. Often there are hot mince pies too.

At three o'clock many people in Britain turn on their televisions because the Queen says 'Happy Christmas' to everyone. A lot of people go for a walk in the afternoon or play with their new games.

In the evening, people eat cold meat, and Christmas cake (a kind of fruit cake) but they are usually not very hungry because of their big dinner.

26 December is called Boxing Day (Saint Stephen's Day in Ireland). It is a holiday for many people, but a lot of shops open on this day. In the nineteenth century, rich people gave boxes of presents to their workers on Boxing Day. Now people enjoy eating, drinking, and watching television at home, or going out to watch some sport.

Another British Christmas tradition is the pantomime. A pantomime is a kind of play with a children's story (like *Cinderella* or *Aladdin*) and lots of music and songs. There is usually a man who wears women's clothes and plays an old woman. 'She' is not very beautiful, but she is usually very funny. Children like pantomimes because they can laugh, sing, shout, and make lots of noise. They often go with their school or family.

The Christmas season ends on the twelfth day after 25 December, which is 6 January. Most people take down their Christmas trees and decorations by this date, and some people think that it is unlucky to do this after 6 January.

But after Christmas the next festival comes very quickly. Soon it is 31 December. It is New Year's Eve – and then a new year of seasons and celebrations begins.

A pantomime at Christmas

GLOSSARY

barbecue a party where you cook food on a fire outside
become to begin to be something
beer a strong, brown-coloured alcoholic drink
cake a sweet food made from flour, eggs, sugar, and butter
celebrate to do something to show that you are happy because it is a special day; **celebration** (*n*)
century a time of one hundred years
champagne a French wine with a lot of bubbles
chief the leader of a group of people
Christian someone who follows the teachings of Jesus Christ; **Christianity** the religion that follows Jesus Christ
coal a hard black substance that comes from under the ground and that is burnt to give heat
colony a country that is ruled by another country
concert music played for a lot of people
culture the customs, ideas, and way of life of a group of people
decorate to make something look nicer by adding beautiful things to it; **decoration** (*n*)
emperor a man who rules a group of countries
fall in love with to begin to love somebody
festival a time when people celebrate something
game something that you play that has rules, e.g. football, tennis
ghost a kind of spirit
god a spirit that people believe has power over them and nature
goddess a female god
government a group of people who control a country
grow to get bigger; to plant something in the ground and look after it
gunpowder a powder used to make guns or fireworks explode
honey a sweet food that is made by bees
Houses of Parliament the buildings where the British government meets

joke (play a joke on)   to do something to another person to make people laugh

kind   a group of things that are the same in some way

message   words that one person sends to another

mix (*n & v*)   to put different things together to make something new

pagan   belonging to a religion that is older than Christianity

park   a large place with trees and gardens where people can go to walk, play games etc.

part   one of the pieces of something

pie   a kind of food made of meat, fruit, or vegetables together with pastry (flour, butter, and water)

plot   a secret plan to do something bad

programme   something that you watch on television

rabbit   a small animal with soft fur and long ears

race   a competition to see who can do something the fastest

religion   believing in a god or gods, and the things you do in connection with this

service   a meeting in a church with prayers and singing

spice   a small part of a plant that you put in food to make it taste good

spirit   the form of a dead person, which you can feel but cannot see

stocking   a long sock

tax   money that you have to pay to the government

torture   to hurt someone in order to make them give you information

tradition   something that people have done for a long time; **traditional** (*adj*)

war   fighting between armies of different countries

war memorial   a stone that is built to make people remember soldiers who died in a war

witch   a woman who can do magic things

Seasons and Celebrations

ACTIVITIES

ACTIVITIES

Before Reading

1 This book is about seasons and celebrations. Which of these things do you think you are going to read about? Tick nine boxes.

☐ songs   ☐ homework
☐ fires   ☐ church
☐ flowers   ☐ planes
☐ storms   ☐ food
☐ soldiers   ☐ presents
☐ cards   ☐ horses
☐ suitcases   ☐ parties

2 Read the back cover of the book, and the introduction on the first page. How much do you know now about celebrations? Are these sentences true (T) or false (F)?

1 Remembrance Day is a new celebration.
2 People celebrate Easter in the winter.
3 Pancakes are a kind of food.
4 There are a lot of new young plants and animals in the autumn.
5 People have barbecues on the Fourth of July.
6 There were no celebrations before Christianity.

ACTIVITIES

While Reading

**Read Chapters 1 and 2. Match the beginnings and the
endings of the sentences.**

1 Easter and Christmas are old festivals that . . .

2 At special times like Mother's Day . . .

3 In London, a lot of people go to Trafalgar Square . . .

4 *Auld Lang Syne* . . .

5 In Scotland, New Year's Eve . . .

6 Things in the shops are cheaper . . .

7 When Valentine was in prison, he . . .

a) in January.

b) is a song about old friends.

c) fell in love.

d) became Christian festivals.

e) is called Hogmanay.

f) on 31 December in the evening.

g) people often send cards.

**Read Chapter 3. Then match the countries with the
national days.**

1 Scotland	a) Saint George's Day
2 Ireland	b) Waitangi Day
3 New Zealand	c) Saint Andrew's Day
4 England	d) Saint David's Day
5 Wales	e) Saint Patrick's Day

Read Chapters 4 and 5. Choose the best question word for these questions, and then answer them.

What / When / How / Why

1 _____ many days are there in Lent?
2 _____ do people eat on the day before Ash Wednesday?
3 _____ was the old name for the goddess of spring?
4 _____ are there often baby sheep or rabbits on Easter cards?
5 _____ do people eat hot cross buns?
6 _____ long have people celebrated Father's Day?
7 _____ was All Fools' Day?
8 _____ did some people want to buy spaghetti trees in 1957?

Read Chapters 6 and 7. Here are some untrue sentences. Change them into true sentences.

1 The summer solstice is the shortest day of the year.
2 The word solstice comes from the Latin word 'sol', which means moon.
3 The big stones at Avebury and Stonehenge have been there for about five hundred years.
4 The 'Boston Coffee Party' in 1773 was a fight about paying taxes.
5 Americans celebrate Independence Day every year on the Fourth of January.
6 In 1960, Hawaii became the fortieth state of the USA.
7 Hundreds of years ago, people made jack o'lanterns in November to keep the good spirits away.
8 At Halloween, children knock on people's doors and say 'trick or present?'
9 In 1605, Guy Fawkes tried to kill the Queen of England.
10 People in Britain have bonfires on 5 December.

Read Chapters 8 and 9, then circle the correct words in each sentence.

1 In the UK, people are silent for two minutes at *ten / eleven* o'clock on 11 November.

2 Many people wear red paper *poppies / roses* on Remembrance Day.

3 In 1915, thousands of young soldiers from Australia and *New Zealand / China* died in Turkey.

4 The Pilgrim Fathers were a group of *Spanish / English* people who sailed to America in 1620.

5 The Wampanoag started living in North America *before / after* the Pilgrim Fathers arrived.

6 In the USA, Thanksgiving Day is near the end of *October / November*.

Read Chapters 10 and 11, then complete the sentences with these words. (Use each word once.)

August, Bethlehem, biggest, cards, Caribbean, Carnival, carols, Christmas, decorations, immigrants, million, San Francisco, thousand

1 The Notting Hill _____ is in London at the end of _____. Immigrants from the _____ began it in the 1960s. About a _____ people come to see it every year.

2 The _____ Chinatown in the USA is in _____. A lot of Chinese _____ live there.

3 Jesus was born about two _____ years ago in _____. People remember that special time at _____.

4 At Christmas, people send _____ and presents to their friends and families. They sing _____ and put _____ in their houses.

After Reading

1 Here are two e-mails about different celebrations. Complete them using the words below (one word for each gap). The subjects and dates also need words from the list.

closed, dancing, December, decorations, Eve, face, fireworks, Halloween, holiday, midnight, October, orange, party, pumpkin, spirits, streets

---

○○○　　　　　　　🔲🔷🔘🔳🔘🔺　　　　　　○

Subject: New Year's _____　　　Time: 23.30　Date: 31 _____

Hello from Edinburgh!
There are thousands of people in the _____. Everyone is singing and _____. There are a lot of _____, too. It's very noisy! In half an hour it will be _____. Everyone is excited! Nobody will go to work tomorrow – it's a _____, and all the banks and shops will be _____. Everyone will stay in bed!
Bye! Tim

○○○　　　　　　　🔲🔷🔘🔳🔘🔺　　　　　　○

Subject: _____　　　Time: 19.45　Date: 31 _____

Hi!
I'm staying with a family in New York. The children are having a _____ tonight. They've dressed as witches and ghosts – they say it keeps the bad _____ away! There are a lot of _____ in the house, too – they're black and _____. Outside the door there's a strange light. Someone has cut a _____ in the side of a _____, and they've put a light in it!
See you!
Tania

2 Find these words in the word search below, and draw lines through them. The words go from left to right and top to bottom.

apples, bonnet, carols, Christmas, decorations, Easter, fools, harvest, pancake, pantomimes, pumpkin, Thanksgiving

T	H	A	N	K	S	G	I	V	I	N	G
P	A	N	T	O	M	I	M	E	S	B	E
M	R	Y	F	C	E	A	S	T	E	R	B
V	V	A	O	A	P	P	L	E	S	L	O
D	E	C	O	R	A	T	I	O	N	S	N
E	S	N	L	O	P	U	M	P	K	I	N
T	T	I	S	L	P	A	N	C	A	K	E
C	H	R	I	S	T	M	A	S	N	E	T

Put the words into groups under these three headings.

SPRING	AUTUMN	WINTER
_____	_____	_____
_____	_____	_____
_____	_____	_____
_____	_____	_____

Now write down all the letters that do not have lines through them, beginning with the first line and going across each line to the end. You now have 13 letters, which make a sentence of 3 words.

1 What is the sentence?
2 Where do you think you will see it, and when?

3 Here is a new photo for the book. Find the best place in
   the book to put the picture, and answer these questions.

   The picture goes on page ___.
   1 What can you see in the photo?
   2 What date is it?
   3 What are the children doing?
   4 Do you think it is morning or evening? Why?

   Now write a caption for the picture.

Caption: _____

4 What happens in your country at these times?

1 the beginning of the new year
2 your national day
3 Mother's Day or Father's Day (or a festival like these)
4 the change of seasons (for example, the beginning of spring, or the middle of summer)

Write two or three sentences about each festival. Try to answer questions like these:

- How do people celebrate? Do they have parties in their houses, or in the streets?
- Do people send cards or presents? Do they go to church, or any other special place?
- Do people eat special food?

5 Do you agree or disagree with these sentences? Explain why.

	AGREE	DISAGREE
1 People spend too much money at Christmas and other festivals.	☐	☐
2 We have too many holidays and festivals in my country.	☐	☐
3 It's important to remember people who died in wars.	☐	☐
4 Fireworks are dangerous – it's wrong to sell them to children.	☐	☐

ABOUT THE AUTHOR

Jackie Maguire was born in Worcester, England, but emigrated to Calgary, Canada as a child. She studied for a bachelor's degree in sociology, and worked in courts and prisons before moving into public education and teaching English. She did a study of teaching English in prisons for her master's degree. After her first teaching job in Chicoutimi, Quebec, she taught in Turku (Finland), Tokyo (Japan), Bristol (England) and Dubai (UAE).

Two of the things Jackie loved most about travelling to different countries were going to local festivals and sampling the local food. This inspired her to share the traditions and dishes of her own country with foreign students, so she designed and ran a popular course on making traditional British dishes.

Her favourite season was spring, especially in the countryside. One of her best-loved times of the year was Easter when the spring flowers are out and the lambs are in the fields . . . closely followed by a good bonfire night party with barbecued sausages and a cup of steaming hot soup . . . and Christmas shopping in old English towns with all the Christmas lights on.

Besides travelling with her journalist husband, Jackie's interests included cooking, watching films from around the world, being part of a reading group, doing yoga, and swimming in the sea (if it was warm enough!). She also tried hot air ballooning and scuba-diving but generally preferred to keep her feet on the ground.

Jackie rewrote *Seasons and Celebrations* for this new edition with her usual energy and enthusiasm, and was looking forward to its publication. However, Jackie died in 2007, after a long and brave fight against illness.

OXFORD BOOKWORMS LIBRARY

Classics • Crime & Mystery • Factfiles • Fantasy & Horror
Human Interest • Playscripts • Thriller & Adventure
True Stories • World Stories

The OXFORD BOOKWORMS LIBRARY provides enjoyable reading in English, with a wide range of classic and modern fiction, non-fiction, and plays. It includes original and adapted texts in seven carefully graded language stages, which take learners from beginner to advanced level. An overview is given on the next pages.

All Stage 1 titles are available as audio recordings, as well as over eighty other titles from Starter to Stage 6. All Starters and many titles at Stages 1 to 4 are specially recommended for younger learners. Every Bookworm is illustrated, and Starters and Factfiles have full-colour illustrations.

The OXFORD BOOKWORMS LIBRARY also offers extensive support. Each book contains an introduction to the story, notes about the author, a glossary, and activities. Additional resources include tests and worksheets, and answers for these and for the activities in the books. There is advice on running a class library, using audio recordings, and the many ways of using Oxford Bookworms in reading programmes. Resource materials are available on the website <www.oup.com/elt/bookworms>.

The *Oxford Bookworms Collection* is a series for advanced learners. It consists of volumes of short stories by well-known authors, both classic and modern. Texts are not abridged or adapted in any way, but carefully selected to be accessible to the advanced student.

You can find details and a full list of titles in the *Oxford Bookworms Library Catalogue* and *Oxford English Language Teaching Catalogues*, and on the website <www.oup.com/elt/bookworms>.

THE OXFORD BOOKWORMS LIBRARY
GRADING AND SAMPLE EXTRACTS

STARTER • 250 HEADWORDS

present simple – present continuous – imperative –
can/cannot, must – *going to* (future) – simple gerunds …

Her phone is ringing – but where is it?

Sally gets out of bed and looks in her bag. No phone. She looks under the bed. No phone. Then she looks behind the door. There is her phone. Sally picks up her phone and answers it. ***Sally's Phone***

STAGE 1 • 400 HEADWORDS

… past simple – coordination with *and, but, or* –
subordination with *before, after, when, because, so* …

I knew him in Persia. He was a famous builder and I worked with him there. For a time I was his friend, but not for long. When he came to Paris, I came after him – I wanted to watch him. He was a very clever, very dangerous man. ***The Phantom of the Opera***

STAGE 2 • 700 HEADWORDS

… present perfect – *will* (future) – *(don't) have to, must not, could* –
comparison of adjectives – simple *if* clauses – past continuous –
tag questions – *ask/tell* + infinitive …

While I was writing these words in my diary, I decided what to do. I must try to escape. I shall try to get down the wall outside. The window is high above the ground, but I have to try. I shall take some of the gold with me – if I escape, perhaps it will be helpful later. ***Dracula***

STAGE 3 • 1000 HEADWORDS

… should, may – present perfect continuous – *used to* – past perfect
– causative – relative clauses – indirect statements …

Of course, it was most important that no one should see Colin, Mary, or Dickon entering the secret garden. So Colin gave orders to the gardeners that they must all keep away from that part of the garden in future. *The Secret Garden*

STAGE 4 • 1400 HEADWORDS

… past perfect continuous – passive (simple forms) –
would conditional clauses – indirect questions –
relatives with *where/when* – gerunds after prepositions/phrases …

I was glad. Now Hyde could not show his face to the world again. If he did, every honest man in London would be proud to report him to the police. *Dr Jekyll and Mr Hyde*

STAGE 5 • 1800 HEADWORDS

… future continuous – future perfect –
passive (modals, continuous forms) –
would have conditional clauses – modals + perfect infinitive …

If he had spoken Estella's name, I would have hit him. I was so angry with him, and so depressed about my future, that I could not eat the breakfast. Instead I went straight to the old house. *Great Expectations*

STAGE 6 • 2500 HEADWORDS

… passive (infinitives, gerunds) – advanced modal meanings –
clauses of concession, condition

When I stepped up to the piano, I was confident. It was as if I knew that the prodigy side of me really did exist. And when I started to play, I was so caught up in how lovely I looked that I didn't worry how I would sound. *The Joy Luck Club*

BOOKWORMS · FACTFILES · STAGE 2
Ireland
TIM VICARY

There are many different Irelands. There is the Ireland of peaceful rivers, green fields, and beautiful islands. There is the Ireland of song and dance, pubs and theatres – the country of James Joyce, Bob Geldof, and Riverdance. And there is the Ireland of guns, fighting, death, and the hope of peace. Come with us and visit all of these Irelands – and many more . . .

BOOKWORMS · FACTFILES · STAGE 2
Rainforests
ROWENA AKINYEMI

Deep rivers, tall trees, strange animals, beautiful flowers – this is the rainforest. Burning trees, thick smoke, new roads and cities, dead animals, people without homes – this is the rainforest too. To some people the rainforests mean beautiful places that you can visit; to others they mean trees that they can cut down and sell.

Between 1950 and 2000 half of the world's rainforests disappeared. While you read these words, somewhere in the world people are cutting down rainforest trees. What are these wonderful places that we call rainforests – and is it too late to save them?

OXFORD BOOKWORMS LIBRARY

Audio Download
Stage 2
Seasons and Celebrations

To download the audio for this title

1 Go to www.oup.com/elt/download

2 Use this code and your email address

Your download code

OXFORD
UNIVERSITY PRESS

ISBN 978-0-19-462187-8

9 780194 621878